ATHENA AND THE OLIVE TREE

WHO IS THE FAIREST ONE OF ALL?

THE WOMAN NO ONE BELIEVED

For Frances Rutherford

ORCHARD BOOKS

96 Leonard Street, London EC2A 4XD

Orchard Books Australia

Unit 31/56 O'Riordan Street, Alexandria NSW 2015

This text was first published in Great Britain in the form of
a gift collection called *The Orchard Book of Greek Gods and Goddesses*,
illustrated by Emma Chichester Clark in 1997.

This edition first published in hardback in Great Britain in 2000

First paperback publication 2001

Text © Geraldine McCaughrean 1997

Illustrations © Tony Ross 2000

The rights of Geraldine McCaughrean to be identified as the author and
Tony Ross as the illustrator of this work have been asserted by them in
accordance with the Copyright, Designs, and Patents Act, 1988.

ISBN 1 84121 893 6 (hardback)

ISBN 1 84121 662 3 (paperback)

1 3 5 7 9 10 8 6 4 2 (hardback)

1 3 5 7 9 10 8 6 4 2 (paperback)

A CIP catalogue record for this book is available
from the British Library.

Printed in Great Britain

ATHENA AND THE OLIVE TREE

WHO IS THE FAIREST ONE OF ALL?
THE WOMAN NO ONE BELIEVED

GERALDINE MCCAUGHREAN
ILLUSTRATED BY TONY ROSS

ORCHARD BOOKS

ATHENA AND THE OLIVE TREE

Zeus's headache got worse and worse, until one day he said, "My head is splitting!" And he was right.

A great throbbing crest swelled across the crown on his head, and when he smacked his fist against it, it split open. Out rose...a woman.

She was fully grown, fully dressed, fully armed. In fact she was clad in armour, with helmet, shield and spear. And she came into the world along a chute of light so dazzling that, for a time, no one in the courts of Heaven could move or speak or think, except to think, "A new goddess has been born today."

The disc of Heaven and the disc of Earth trembled like cymbals struck together, and Helios stopped the sun chariot stock-still in the sky, to stare. The goddess's mouth was open, and a cry – a battle cry – set the fish shimmering in the sea far below.

Then the warrior woman closed her mouth, struck the pavements of Olympus three times with the butt of her spear, and freed the gods from their trance, like sleepwalkers startled awake.

Her eyes were a silver grey, and when she looked at her father, Zeus knew at once how long she had lain nestled against his brain, unborn. "You are the daughter of Metis, my first wife," he said, his amazement mixed with delight. Suddenly the prophecy that Metis's child would be greater than him no longer seemed such a terrible threat to Zeus: he had always imagined a son...

So Zeus did not open his mouth and swallow her, as he had swallowed her mother. He did not banish her from Heaven. In fact, from the day of her birth, she was his dearest child: Pallas Athena.

"'Dear grey eyes', he calls her," said
Poseidon, as sour and surly as ever among
the draughty currents of the deep sea.
"The others call her 'Mighty', 'Champion',
'The Warlike One', 'Protector of Little
Children!'…'Goddess of the City'. Well,
she won't be goddess of *my* city, and she
needn't think she will!"

By 'his' city, Poseidon meant the new, the marvellous city being built by King Cecrops as a lesson to the world in civilised living. In time it would be home to thousands, with a host of lovely buildings – senate houses, theatres, covered markets and bath-houses. At present it had two rivers and the Acropolis – a hill of resplendent beauty waiting, just waiting to be crowned with a temple.

But to which of the gods would King Cecrops dedicate his perfect city?

"It's only four miles from the sea. Of *course* it must be mine," said Poseidon, striking his trident on the floor of Heaven.

"And yet I would rather like it myself," said the grey-eyed goddess standing beside Zeus's throne.

Zeus wanted Athena to have it, but thought it best to ask King Cecrops to choose. After all, the man had taught Humankind how to worship the gods properly, so he would clearly make a wise choice.

11

And *he* could take the blame, rather than Zeus, for offending either Poseidon or Athena. Cecrops was sent for and asked, "Which god shall be patron of your new city, and give it its name, and have their temple on the Hill of the Acropolis? Shall it be Poseidon or grey-eyed Athena?"

Cecrops plucked at his lower lip and considered. He could see the barbs of Poseidon's trident twinkling, see the eagle glisten on the breastplate of Athena's armour "I shall dedicate the city to whomsoever grants it the most useful present."

Hardly were the words spoken before
Poseidon drove off full tilt in his turtleshell
chariot. He split the sea asunder as he
entered it, and galloped in frantic circles
around the amphitheatre of the Undersea,
so as to set the oceans spinning.

Up from his stables came his white-maned storm horses, clashing their silver hoofs, stampeding over the sea's surface with arched necks and flaring nostrils.

Choosing the very finest of his steeds, Poseidon moulded its watery bulk into solid horseflesh, and let it ashore on an Aegean beach – the world's first horse of flesh and blood.

"This beast I give you, Cecrops, and all its four-footed foals for evermore. From now on, your merchants may transport their goods in horse-drawn wagons, your soldiers

charge into battle on horseback, your farmers plough their fields without a pick!"

Cecrops stood and clapped. He could imagine no better present. And behind him the gods and goddesses of Olympus, ranged like the judges at a trial, were clearly just as impressed. Poseidon's city it would be.

15

Then, all of a sudden, Athena was standing on the crest of the hill of the Acropolis, spear in hand.

No, no. This time it was not a spear she was holding, but a little tree. As she thrust it into the ground, it grew and spread its branches – leaves the shape of a spearhead, and fruit as green and black as grapes.

"This is the olive tree," she said. "You may eat its fruit or crush it and make oil – oil to cook by, to light your houses, to flavour your meat and bread. Its leaves are soft to sleep on, its shade as cool as water at noon."

And once Cecrops had tasted the olive, he had to agree that life would never be the same again for anyone whose land contained the olive tree.

"The name of my city will be Athena," said King Cecrops, "and the temple on the Acropolis shall be the Parthenon, temple to the immortal maiden Athena!"

A rumble shook the assembly of dignitaries which seemed to come from far beneath the Earth, but which really came from Poseidon's throat. He growled the growl of a ship foundering, of a sea monster grating its teeth, of the boulders at the bottom of the sea grinding each other to sand.

Then his hand jerked and his trident flew – and struck the hill of the Acropolis like the flank of a whale.

Out of the wound
spurted salt water –
not just a spring
but a fountain, a
geyser, a gusher of
seawater pluming
into the sky then
falling back on
the heads of the
assembled immortals.
Soon the ground was
muddy, the puddles
joined into lakes, and the

whole coastal plain disappeared beneath
a flood which stretched all the way to
the sea. Huge waves rolled in off the five
oceans, and moved on unhindered over
the Thracian Plain, submerging crops,
destroying houses, drowning animals
who could not reach higher ground.

Huddled together at the top of the Acropolis, their arms round each others' waists, the Olympians and King Cecrops looked out over the greatest flood in the history of their world, and wondered at the jealousy of the sea god.

"Enough! You are a sullen and peevish bully, brother!" declared Zeus, pointing his aegis at the flood and drying it up in great twisting columns of steam. "You shall pay back the people of Athens for this wanton destruction of yours! In place of soft waves, you shall live for a time among hard, dry stones, and in place of your cold deeps, you may labour a while in the hot sun to earn gold as they have to do each day!"

And for sending the flood, Poseidon was made to spend seven years building the walls of a city. Not Athens. It was a citadel with a wall twenty metres high and five metres thick of shining white stone. No weapon must breach it, no attacker scale it. It was to be the greatest fortress-city in the world.

It was to be Troy.

WHO IS THE FAIREST ONE OF ALL?

The Race of Gold, the Race of Silver, the Race of Bronze: Zeus made them, then despaired of them. The Race of Iron was no different. Their crops drained the goodness from the land, their fishing plundered the sea, and their cities weighed heavy on the Earth's surface. They cut down trees for firewood, and they made more noise than a pack of apes in a bucket.

So Zeus resolved to *reduce* the number of mortals on the Earth. All it would take would be a single golden apple and the help of the Immortals – though he told them nothing of what he was planning. He gave the golden apple to Eris, god of strife, and Eris took it to a wedding.

All the gods and goddesses were there, the naiads and nereids, the dryads, the satyrs and the centaurs. Dionysus had brought the wine, and no one begrudged the bride and groom an eternity of happiness. They had left at home their petty rivalries, and brought instead their sweetest smiles to the wedding.

No one saw Eris take out the apple and drop it casually to the ground. But everyone saw the apple.

For the fairest, said the inscription.

"How kind," said Hera, smiling round her in a queenly way. "Oh, but surely – it's meant for me," said Aphrodite, goddess of love, brushing her hair back coyly. "I mean, I presume..."

"You presume too much. You always did," said Athena, putting her foot on the apple so that Aphrodite should not pick it up. "I claim the apple."

The wedding guests murmured their own opinions. Then they all began to quarrel about who was fairest.

"Zeus the Shining shall decide!" declared Hera, already thinking how best to make up her husband's mind for him.

But Zeus refused. "Judge between my wife and my daughters? Impossible! Ask a mortal to choose. He'll be impartial. And let the most handsome decide the most fair. Which *is* the handsomest youth on Earth, would you say?"

On that no one disagreed. In every alcove and bower, goddesses, nymphs and mermaids – even the bride – sighed the name "Paris!"

Paris was the Prince of Troy – an alarmingly good-looking boy who had not yet fallen in love. Hermes, messenger of the gods, was sent to fetch him.

One moment he was alone, fishing on the seashore, the next he was blinking at the brightness of the Cloudy Citadel. Before him sat the three most powerful goddesses in the world, carefully arranging the drapery of their gowns. "Look, don't touch," Hermes whispered in his ear. "And above all, Paris, listen. It may be to your advantage."

As Paris passed in front of Hera's throne with its golden eagles, she bared her teeth in a smile and whispered, "Decide in my favour and I shall make you the ruler of empires." "Thank you," said Paris. "How kind."

As he passed in front of Athena, she struck the pavement of Heaven with the butt of her spear so loudly that Paris started. "I see it now," she whispered, glaring at him with her solemn grey eyes. "I, goddess of battle, see the  crown of a dozen glorious victories round your brow! What battles won't I win for the man who proclaims me fairest of all!"

"Thank you," said Paris, and gave her such a dazzling smile that she dropped her helmet.

By the time Paris reached Aphrodite, goddess of love, he was learning the rules of the game. "What will *you* give me if I award the apple to you?" he said.

"What every mortal man wants most,"
she murmured, puckering her fulsome lips.
"The love of the loveliest woman on Earth."

Paris did not hesitate. He laid the apple in
Aphrodite's lap...then ran for his life as
sandals and spears came flying after him.

So Aphrodite won the apple, and she was true to her word. She gave Paris the love of the most lovely woman on Earth: Helen. There was something she failed to mention, however: Helen was already married.

But then, that was Zeus's plan. When fair Helen laid eyes on Paris, she fell in love instantly and completely. Her husband was forgotten: all questions of right and wrong dissolved as she fled across the sea to the home of her handsome prince. As she fled to Troy.

In his rage and grief, her husband called on the King of Greece for help. The King called on his friends and allies to join forces with him and go after Helen – to make Paris and Troy pay for stealing her away. An army of thousands mustered their fleets of fast black ships, and prayed to the gods for success.

Now the gods, too, took sides.

"Oh yes," said vengeful Hera, "I'll help defeat Paris."

"No," said Aphrodite, "Paris must have his Helen. I'm for Troy."

"So am I!" said Apollo. "There's a princess in Troy I'm particularly fond of."

"Well, I shan't rest till Troy is in ruins and the Trojans face down in the sea," said surly Poseidon. "I asked them for wages for building their precious walls. They told me they had a war to pay for, no money to spare. I'll make them pay for that."

For Athena the choice was harder. Troy, like Athens, was dedicated to her – its greatest treasure was a statue of her which the Trojans called the Luck of Troy. And yet Paris must pay...

All the mortal world took sides in the Wars of Troy. And above them the gods, too, ranged themselves for or against the Trojans or the Greeks.

Zeus looked down from
his seat of power and
watched the Earth
bristle with columns
of marching men.
The nights twinkled
with the fires of
blacksmiths forging
weapons. Shiploads
of horses rode on
the high seas.

It was his chessboard, all set up for the Great Game. With the unwitting help of the gods, the Wars of Troy would go on for years, killing men by the hundred, by the tens of hundreds – and women and children too. The Earth would be eased of the weight of human feet, the fields and woodlands left fallow. Everywhere would be washed clean in a tide of blood.

It was the perfect plan.

THE WOMAN NO ONE BELIEVED

As well as the statue called
the Luck of Troy, the Trojans
had another treasure: Princess Cassandra.
She was so beautiful, even as a child, that
seven generals swore allegiance to the King
of Troy, hoping to win her for a bride
when she was older. She slept in a temple,
so that no one would steal her away.

But it was Apollo's temple. When Apollo saw the sleeping Cassandra, what he saw roused more love in him than he had felt since his little friend Hyacinthus died. "Until you are a woman, Cassandra, and mine," he said. And he bent and kissed her dear little ears.

In his breath he passed her the gift of prophecy, so that when she woke Cassandra was even more of a marvel than before. For she could hear far-off voices talking of things to come. After the war broke out, the King and Queen would often ask her,

"How will this end, Cassandra? How will this dreadful war end?" But the truth still lay far off, like a figure on a roadway still blurred by dust and distance.

When Cassandra was sixteen, in the middle of the war, Apollo came back to claim her. All swagger and bluster and arrogance, he swept into her room and said, "No more waiting! I have come for you!"

"I am honoured, sir, but I've decided to stay unmarried."

"But I'm Apollo the Shining! Apollo the Immortal! Look, here's my lyre!"

"Even so," said Cassandra. "Please go."

"But I love you! I gave you the gift of prophecy! I kissed your ears! I made you what you are today!"

Cassandra blushed. "Oh, was it you? I was asleep. You really should have woken me and asked if I *wanted* your gift... You can take it back if you like."

Apollo was mortified. Never had his love and his presents been spurned so flatly. "A gift from the gods cannot be taken back," he complained. "Kiss, at least!"

40

Cassandra supposed there would be no harm in that. So they kissed. And in his breath, Apollo passed to her a second gift, because he could not take away the first.

"Make your prophecies, Princess," he sneered, pushing her roughly away. "I have made you even more *gifted* than before."

When he had gone, into Cassandra's mind dawned a series of terrible visions: fires and blood, swords and a giant horse, ships and shadows and falling masonry. Her pretty face turned quite pale at the shock.

"Mother! Father! The Greeks are going to win! The Greeks are going to kill you and take me prisoner! I see it all!"

"Hush, hush, child. You don't look well. Lie down. You've had a nightmare. Troy is quite safe," said the King.

"*Troy will burn!*" yelled Cassandra, gripping his cloak. "*Don't you understand? I've seen it burning! Troy will burn!*"

But the wilder Cassandra became, the more the Trojans told themselves, "The Princess has gone mad. How tragic – such beauty tied to such madness." She was cursed, you see. Apollo had cursed her – with Disbelief.

Soon her dark hair was grey with frenzy, her beautiful face haggard and lined. She tore her clothes and ran through the streets seizing hold of passers-by. "The Greeks have a plan! They'll send a horse!" But no one believed her. No one. That was Apollo's revenge for his wounded pride.

After ten years of war, the Greeks built a horse – a great wooden horse, a tribute to Troy, the City of Horses. They left it on the beach, its wooden ears almost as high as the gated arch in Troy's wall. Then they sailed away, and all that was left were the black circles of a thousand campfires.

"Burn it! Burn the horse! It's a trick!" shrieked Cassandra. But by now she was only the ragged madwoman who ran about the streets with straws in her hair and desperation in her eyes.

With ships' hawsers they dragged the wooden horse in through the gates and stood it in the market square, dancing round it, celebrating their sudden and total victory.

"Burn it! Destroy it!" howled Cassandra. *"Can't you hear the soldiers' armour jingling inside? Can't you hear them breathing?"*

But Apollo's curse damned the Trojans as utterly as it had damned Cassandra. They took no notice of her voice below their windows that night. They did not believe her when she said that the fast black ships were even now sailing back into the bay, that twenty Greek warriors were even now climbing down out of the wooden horse, unbarring the gate in the impenetrable wall, letting in the enemy to sack Troy.

It all happened just as she had seen it in her head. The towers fell in flames. The temples were looted. The King and Queen died. Cassandra was taken into slavery.

And all the while, the giant wooden horse looked down with its painted eyes as if to say, "I believed you, Princess. I believed you all along."